Pebble™

Woodland Animals

Woodpeckers

common flicker

by Emily Rose Townsend

Consulting Editor: Gail Saunders-Smith, Ph.D.
Consultant: William John Ripple, Professor
Department of Forest Resources
Oregon State University

Capstone
press
Mankato, Minnesota

Pebble Books are published by Capstone Press
151 Good Counsel Drive, P.O. Box 669, Mankato, Minnesota 56002
http://www.capstonepress.com

1 2 3 4 5 6 09 08 07 06 05 04

Library of Congress Cataloging-in-Publication Data
Townsend, Emily Rose.
    Woodpeckers / by Emily Rose Townsend.
    p. cm.—(Woodland animals)
    Includes bibliographical references (p. 23) and index.
    Contents: Woodpeckers—Woodlands—What woodpeckers do.
    ISBN 0-7368-2070-1 (hardcover)
    1. Woodpeckers—Juvenile literature. [1. Woodpeckers.] I. Title.
QL696.P56T68 2004
598.7'2—dc21   2003011210

Note to Parents and Teachers

The Woodland Animals series supports national science standards
related to life science. This book describes and illustrates
woodpeckers. The photographs support early readers in
understanding the text. The repetition of words and phrases helps
early readers learn new words. This book also introduces early
readers to subject-specific vocabulary words, which are defined in
the Glossary. Early readers may need assistance to read some words
and to use the Table of Contents, Glossary, Read More, Internet
Sites, and Index/Word List sections of the book.

Table of Contents

Woodpeckers

Woodpeckers are birds with long, sharp beaks.

red-headed woodpecker

Woodpeckers have long, sharp tongues.

red-bellied woodpecker

Woodpecker feathers
have many colors
and patterns.

downy woodpecker

areas where woodpeckers live

Woodlands

Woodpeckers live almost everywhere in the world. Most woodpeckers live in woodlands.

12

Woodlands are covered with trees and shrubs. Woodlands are also called forests.

What Woodpeckers Do

Woodpeckers use their sharp claws to climb up and down trees.

pileated woodpecker

Most woodpeckers drill holes in tree trunks with their beaks. Woodpeckers make a drumming sound when they drill.

hairy woodpecker

Woodpeckers eat nuts, seeds, insects, and fruit.

red-bellied woodpecker

Woodpeckers sometimes make nests inside trees.

common flicker

Glossary

beak—the hard part of a bird's mouth

bird—a warm-blooded animal that has feathers and wings and can lay eggs; woodpeckers are birds; there are more than 200 kinds of woodpeckers in the world.

drill—to make a hole; woodpeckers use their sharp beaks to quickly hit tree trunks many times; this action makes holes in tree trunks.

insect—a small animal with a hard outer shell, six legs, three body sections, and two antennas; woodpeckers eat insects.

pattern—a repeated arrangement of colors and shapes

shrub—a plant or bush with woody stems that branch out near the ground

Read More

Butterfield, Moira. *Animals in Trees.* Looking At. Austin, Texas: Raintree Steck-Vaughn, 2000.

Kalz, Jill. *Woodpeckers.* Birds. Mankato, Minn.: Smart Apple Media, 2002.

Murray, Julie. *Woodpeckers.* Animal Kingdom. Edina, Minn.: Abdo, 2003.

Internet Sites

FactHound offers a safe, fun way to find Internet sites related to this book. All of the sites on FactHound have been researched by our staff.

Here's how:

1. Visit *www.facthound.com*
2. Type in this special code **0736820701** for age-appropriate sites. Or enter a search word related to this book for a more general search.
3. Click on the **Fetch It** button.

FactHound will fetch the best sites for you!

Index/Word List

beaks, 5, 17
birds, 5
claws, 15
climb, 15
colors, 9
drill, 17
drumming, 17
eat, 19
feathers, 9

forests, 13
fruit, 19
holes, 17
insects, 19
live, 11
long, 5, 7
nests, 21
nuts, 19
patterns, 9

seeds, 19
sharp, 5,
  7, 15
shrubs, 13
tongues, 7
tree, 13,
  15, 17, 21
woodlands,
  11, 13

Word Count: 85
Early-Intervention Level: 12

Editorial Credits
Mari C. Schuh, editor; Patrick D. Dentinger, designer; Scott Thoms, photo researcher;
   Karen Risch, product planning editor

Photo Credits
Ann & Rob Simpson, 4, 8, 16
Bill Beatty, 6
Brian Gosewisch, cover, 1, 18
Comstock, 12
Corbis, 10
Dwight R. Kuhn, 20
Joe McDonald, 14